The Essential
Girls' Guide to Growing Up

What happens to your Body and Mind

Explanation incl. Skin Care Tips

Puberty Books for Girls age 9-12

Annabel E. Lewis

ISBN: 9798673318515

Table of Contents

Introduction 1

Chapter One: The Dictionary of Words You Need
    to Know 4

Chapter Two: What is Puberty?............................. 8

    Puberty. 8

Chapter Three: What is Happening to Your Body? 13

    You'll Gain Weight and Grow Taller 14

    Your Breasts Will Start to Grow........................ 15

    You'll Start Experiencing Vaginal Discharge ... 18

    You'll Start Growing Body Hair 21

    You're Going to Start Sweating 24

    You're Going to Get Some Acne....................... 25

    You're Going to Start Menstruating 27

Chapter Four: Everything You Need to Know
    About Periods 28

    What is a Period? 29

How Will I Know When My Period is Coming?. 32

How Can I Be Prepared for My Period?............ 34

How to Use a Sanitary Towel 35

How to Use a Tampon 36

What Happens If I Don't Have Tampons or
    Pads? 38

There's Blood on My Underwear / Trousers/
    Pants?! 41

How Do I Track My Periods? 42

Can I Swim on My Period? 43

I Heard Some People Go Crazy on Their
    Period? 44

How Bad is Period Pain?................................... 46

Do Periods Ever Stop? 47

Can I Talk to My Parents About Being on My
    Period? 48

Chapter Five: Understanding Your Mind During
    Puberty 49

Feeling the Pressures of Growing Up 51

How to Deal with Mood Swings........................ 53

You Can Always Get Support 54

Dealing with Sexual Feelings 55

Talking About Masturbation 58

Talking About Body Image 60

A Quick Look into Relationships 65

Chapter Six: How to Look After Yourself During

Puberty 70

Eat as Well as You Can 71

Make Sure You Exercise! 72

Keep a Note of Everything 74

Be Prepared 76

Chapter Seven: How Puberty Affects Your Skin 79

Bonus: Skin Care Tips You Need to Know 82

Why is Looking After Your Skin Important? 83

The Basics of Looking After Your Skin.............. 84

Finding Your 'Skin Type' 87

Avoid Makeup Powders..................................... 89

Be Careful with Your Makeup 90

Think About Your Diet 92

Don't Touch Your Spots! 93

Exfoliate Your Skin!... 96

Use Sunscreen 97

Get Professional Help 98

Final Thoughts 99

Disclaimer.. 102

Introduction

Girls, there comes a point in your life where you're going to look in the mirror and realize something. Something big. Your body is changing. You might find you're a little bit taller than you remember, or perhaps your waist is getting wider. You may find all your body is changing, including your mind and the way you think, and you're wondering what is going on. You may already be going through this, which is why you're reading this book, or maybe you've heard stories from your parents or girls at school who are going through this big, crazy time called puberty.

Right off the bat, I'm here to tell you that puberty isn't as big and as scary as it may seem. You've probably heard stories about what is happening to your body and your brain during this time. Still, it's really nothing to worry about. All that is happening is that you're turning from a kid into a teenager, and eventually onto an adult. Every girl in the human race goes through these changes, so you don't need to think for a moment you're alone in this. You're not.

I went through it. Your friends will go through it. Your mom, your aunt, and your grandma went through it. However, while puberty and the way your body changes are very natural, it's always a good idea to understand what's going on. Your body and brain are changing in ways that haven't happened before, and it's going to feel weird.

Some days you're going to look at yourself in the mirror and love yourself, and other days you're not. It's just how life works. What I'm going to do within the pages of this book is go through what puberty is and how it will affect you. You can then learn everything you need to know to be prepared for these changes, meaning that your puberty won't be as scary or as worrying as it may be already.

In the following chapters, we're going to talk about what puberty actually is (and it's nothing to be ashamed of). We'll cover what this means for your body, what periods are, and how both your mind and body are going to change along the way. We'll also talk about how to deal with it all. Then, as a bit of bonus, I'll even share some of the best skin care tips out there to help you look at feel your best.

Because if you're feeling good in your own skin, there's nothing in life that can stop you! Let's get into it.

Chapter One: The Dictionary of Words You Need to Know

Throughout this book, I'm going to be using a lot of different words and phrases. Some of these words you may have heard before, and some of them may be completely new. Don't worry if you don't understand all these words and terms. You'll get to know them as you grow up and have your own life experiences!

However, just so you have some idea what I'm talking about, here's a dictionary of all the words you need to know. Don't forget you can come back to this book and this table at any time. So, if you need to know what a word means, come back here and look it up!

Let this be your first guide into the words of puberty you need to know!

Puberty	The time in your life you'll go through between the ages of 9 and 17 where your body turns from a child into an adult.
Hormones	A chemical or substance in the body that makes things happen, such as causing your body and muscles to grow.
Period	The name of the process where your body will release the eggs and lining of your womb out of your vagina once a month.
Menstruation	Another word given to the process of having a period.
Acne	A skin condition that causes you to have lots of spots and pimples over your skin.

	This can happen anywhere, all over your body.
Sebum	A natural body oil that comes out of the glands in your skin and can cause acne.
Mental Heath	A term that talks about how you feel, whether you're happy or sad, angry, depressed, anxious, stressed, or content.
Sex	Talks about the act of having physical, intimate contact between you and another person.
Gender	Whether you are a boy or a girl
Discharge	A fluid that comes out of your vagina, usually thick and white, that helps the vagina stay clean and healthy.

Sanitary Products	Products you'll buy and use to help deal with your period by soaking up blood and allowing you to get on with your day.
Tampon	A type of sanitary product that is inserted into your vagina.
Sanitary Pad (Towel)	A type of sanitary product that sits on the outside of your vagina and doesn't go inside you.
Genitals (Genital area)	The private part of boys and girls that include the sexual reproduction organs. This includes breasts, your vagina, and a male penis.
Estrogen	The female reproduction hormone which causes puberty to happen!

Chapter Two: What is Puberty?

Puberty.

It's a word you've probably heard loads about at school and maybe even spoken to your parents about. Now it's important to remember that when you're hearing about periods and puberty and everything from your friends or from TV, there's no guarantee that what you're hearing is actually true. I remember hearing a story about a girl how had a period and was sick for a year. That didn't happen, but I believed it at the time, which made my time in puberty much scarier. Until I found out it wasn't real. I was worrying over nothing.

So, let me tell you the facts, so you know exactly what we're talking about. Puberty is the time in a kid's life when their body prepares itself and changes so you can reproduce, basically meaning you can have children of your own. This change happens in both boys and girls, although girls tend to go through the changes earlier than boys.

If you're wondering what causes these changes, then know that it's your body releasing a hormone known as Estrogen that makes all these changes happen. Don't worry too much about the science behind it all, as you'll learn this in school during your upcoming years. If you are interested, a simple way to look at it is this.

Your body is made up of lots of different chemicals, like water. Every living being in the world has hormones, including your pets. They are used to control things like how much sugar you have in your body, making your blood keep you alive, and turning food into energy that helps you do things. In this case, the hormone known as Estrogen puts your body into puberty!

Since your body is physically getting ready to have the ability to have children, lots of changes are going to happen, many of which we're going to talk about in the following chapters in detail; but just to give you a little rundown of what to expect;

- You'll grow taller

- You'll put on weight

- Your breasts will develop and grow

- You'll have periods

- You'll grow hair on your body

- You'll experience mood swings

Now don't worry, these changes aren't as bad as they may seem. For example, putting on weight is natural because your breasts will be growing, and you'll grow wider hips, so obviously you're going to put on weight. This doesn't mean you're going to be obese or overweight just because you're going into puberty.

Before we head into detail on what it means to go into puberty, some important key points to remember. First, every single girl goes through puberty, but some girls will have different experiences to others. Your breasts may grow earlier that some other girls. You may even be the first in class to experience this.

Don't worry. Some girls experience these changes early. Some girls experience them later on, sometimes even as late as 13 or 14 years old. Again, don't worry if you're early or late. You will have your experience when you have it, and that's okay. Everyone is different, and we girls have just got to stick together and help each other through.

That is a very important point to remember. Puberty is entirely normal. Just because a girl in your class is growing breasts or getting taller than anyone else in your class, that doesn't make her weird or strange. It's just the time for her to go through these changes. If that girl is you and you're the first one, then don't worry. Every other girl will go through this in no time.

It's all about being as prepared as possible with what's to come.

Chapter Three: What is Happening to Your Body?

Some of the biggest changes to happen to your body when entering and making your way through puberty will happen to your body. Most people agree that puberty lasts around five to eight years, but that's just a rule of thumb. Our bodies are always changing, every single day of our lives. That's just how it is.

However, the biggest changes undoubtedly happen while in puberty, or at least the most notable changes, which we're going to look at throughout this chapter.

You'll Gain Weight and Grow Taller

Probably the clearest change is that you'll put on weight and grow taller. Don't worry, you're not going to become a giant or become overweight; it's just your body turning into an adult body, like your parent or teacher. Think of this way, if you grow taller, then there's already more of you, which is why you put on weight. It's not the kind of weight you put on if you eat a giant pizza.

Normally girls will have their growth spurts earlier than boys, so you can see that happening when you next go to class. If you want the science, most girl bodies will go from 8% body fat to 21% body fat, so it's really not as dramatic as you may think, and you definitely don't need to diet to lose the weight. This is known as 'good fat,' and it's all very healthy because it's your body getting ready to have periods in a healthy way.

You'll also find that your hips around your stomach will start to get curvier, which is also very normal. Hips grow wider, so when you decide to have a baby in later life, your body will be able to hold the weight of the baby inside you.

Your Breasts Will Start to Grow

It doesn't matter whether you're a girl who loves the idea of having breasts or are a bit worried by them; they're going to happen anyway. You may worry that your breasts are growing too quickly during puberty, or they're not growing fast enough. Yes, I know, it's hard to not compare your breast sizes with the other girls in your class and your friends.

Remember what we said in chapter one; every girl goes through their own experience at their own speed.

You may not grow breasts for years, and then all of a sudden, over a few months, they suddenly grow and catch up with everyone else. On the other hand, you may grow breasts really early and have yours grow before any other girl does, and that's okay too. It will all happen in its own time, so it's important not to judge anyone else.

What is actually happening when your breasts grow is that your milk ducts inside your breasts are growing, so you can feed your baby milk when you decide to have one. Although your breasts may start to grow at the age of 11, they will continue to grow all the way up until you're 17 or 18 years old, and some girls will keep going all the way up until they are 20.

If you look at yourself in the mirror, you may also notice that your nipples will start to change at the same time. You'll probably find they change color, either going pink or brown, and some may change direction and turn inwards or grow upwards. Some girls will also have hair grow around their nipples. These things are completely normal and experienced by every girl, even if they don't admit it.

If you're feeling a little worried about how your breasts are growing, you can either talk to your mom about it or see a school guidance counselor or teacher. It may be scary to talk to them at first, but these women have all gone through the exact same thing already and will be able to help you can stress-free.

When your breasts to do start to grow, this means it's time to get a bra! Getting your first bra is a very exciting time because it's one of the early signs that you're becoming an adult woman! However, if you're feeling self-conscious about getting a bra, especially if you're one of the first girls in your class to get a bra. Remember, everyone will be catching up with you in the next couple of months and years.

If you find people, perhaps your mom, are making a big deal out of getting you your first bra, you don't need to worry. She's just very excited about you becoming a woman since mothers find it very exciting to see their daughters growing up and becoming adults. She's just really happy and proud of you and how much you're growing up!

You'll Start Experiencing Vaginal Discharge

I remember when I saw my discharge for the first time. I was about 12 years old, and I took my pants off, and there was this yucky white stuff there, and I screamed and cried for a few days because I thought I was really ill. Then, once I had calmed down a bit, I realized that this was discharge that my mom had been telling me about, and it was really nothing to worry about.

Vaginal discharge is what your vagina produces naturally to help keep it moist and clean. The vagina is a very delicate part of a girl's body and will remain this way throughout your life. Your body is an amazing thing because it can clean itself and help you stay healthy down there, which is very important for fighting potential infections and bacteria.

So, when you're getting changed and notice sticky, white fluid in your underpants, don't worry since it's completely normal. Just make sure you keep up with washing yourself and making sure you wear clean underwear every single day.

This discharge can sometimes have an odor to it. However, this is only noticeable if you really try and smell it, and no one else will smell it as you go through your day or at school or anywhere like this. If you do get worried about the smell, you can just bathe with soap, and it will go away, but it's really nothing to worry about.

Having discharge like this can give you little problems, especially if it becomes irritated or itchy. Sometimes it will change from white into a dark yellow or even green color or smell a lot stronger than usual. If this happens, and it will probably happen once or twice throughout your life, just go and see a doctor since you've probably got a vaginal infection.

Again, these naturally happen, especially if you're just trying to figure out your body and learn how to look after it. The doctor will simply diagnose the problem and will probably give you some medicine to make it better and to treat the infection.

You may be wondering if you need to keep your vagina clean or not, especially since it's self-cleaning with discharge. While you don't need to keep it clean, it is important to wash your vagina, just to make sure. Also, avoid wearing plastic-backed underwear, especially while you're on your period because they stop the air from circulating.

This can cause your vagina to warm up and collect excessive moisture, leading to bacteria building up and eventually leading to infections. These should be avoided at all costs!

You'll Start Growing Body Hair

One of the scariest changes your body will go through is when you start to grow body hair. When this happened to me, I began to freak out because I always thought boys were supposed to grow hair and not me. I thought I was turning into a boy! Obviously, this isn't what is happening, and girls growing hair on parts of their body is completely normal.

You'll generally find hair in places like in your armpits or under your arms, on your genital area, and on the top of your lip (your upper lip). If you have hair already or your legs and your arms, you may find this hair will get a little darker, and sometimes a bit thicker.

All of these places are completely normal. It's worth pointing out that the hair on your genital area will be a little different from the rest of your hair. It's usually much darker here and will become curly with time. It's usually a lot thicker here than other parts of your body, and it may spread down your inner thigh and to your leg. Don't worry, this is just what happens; it's only worth noting that there is a difference, and not all body hair is the same.

The only hair you'll want to be concern about is if you have hair growing on your chin or your chest. You know those hormones we were talking about? Well, if you have hair growing on either your chin, your chest, or both, then you may have a hormone imbalance, which will be sorted out with a visit to your doctor.

However, don't strain your eyes trying to look for hairs here. You're going to have small hairs naturally here, and around your nipples, so don't worry unless a lot is growing.

You may want to start shaving some of the hair on your body, especially visible hair on your armpits or upper lip. The hair on your body is the hair on your body, and you can do whatever you want with it. Many women will indeed choose to shave their faces and their armpits, and that's okay because it's their choice to do so.

There is also a growing movement for girls not to shave their armpits because many women in the past felt like they had to do it because the world told them too. The most important thing to remember here is that you can do whatever you want, and it's completely your choice whether you shave or not.

Maybe you want to try it and see how you feel. Perhaps you'll keep shaving, or perhaps you just don't care about it. Feeling either of these ways is absolutely fine because it's about doing whatever makes you happy.

If you decide you want to shave, then make sure you're using a razor or electric shaver designed for women (ask your mom to help you get one). Also, use water and soap to clean the area you're shaving, so you don't let any dirt get into your skin. It's also important to have your own shaver or razor and that you don't share or borrow with anybody else!

You're Going to Start Sweating

It may seem gross to thinking about sweating all the time, even when you're not running around or exercising. Still, it's really nothing to worry about. Again, sweating while you're going through puberty is just a natural part of the process. However, one thing you need to think about is staying clean and washing regularly.

While sweating itself during puberty isn't a big deal, it can cause body odor, which may be something that worries you. This happens when your body sweat mixes with bacteria but can be cleaned up by washing with soap every day. You can have a bath or shower; it's really up to you! Just make sure you're using deodorant soap and use antiperspirant sprays or roll-ons throughout the day.

You may find your feet and your armpits become the sweatiest. The best thing to do is make sure you're wearing clothes that either let your skin breathe or cotton (especially cotton socks) that soak up any moisture and will make it a lot more comfortable for you to get through the day.

On your feet, make sure you're also wearing fabric shoes and not metal or plastic ones since this will make your feet sweat more!

You're Going to Get Some Acne

Perhaps the biggest bad point about puberty is getting acne. Everyone gets acne in one form or another, and this can be in all kinds. Whiteheads, blackheads, and pimples. They are all caused by the rush of hormones in your body that are causing puberty to happen in the first place.

I want to start by saying that worrying about your skin isn't something you need to do. Yes, there's a bit of a stigma to having spots, and it doesn't feel nice. When I had my first outbreak, I thought it was the end of the world, and I wasn't ever going to feel pretty or beautiful again.

But, in time, this acne passes, and before you know it, you'll be a gorgeous and beautiful adult. Towards the end of this book, I'm going to be sharing with you some of the best skin care tips you need to know to help clear up your skin, so you can make it through puberty while feeling good about you.

Don't worry, I know what it's like. While what you look like feels so important, and when you don't feel yourself, it's a really horrible feeling, other people will say that looks don't matter, and it's about being a kind person that really counts. It's what's on the inside that matters. This is true, but, as I know, it doesn't really stop you from feeling any less bad towards yourself.

With that, you can find my quick skincare tips at the end of the book. Acne, like most other signs of puberty we've spoken about, will be different for each girl and boy. Some days you may have really bad acne, and some days you may have none. It really feels random, so you'll just have to see what happens to you.

It's just that most important thing to remember that everyone gets acne. Everyone goes through puberty, so don't judge or laugh at other girls who may have it bad. Within months, you may get terrible acne yourself, and you won't want people laughing at you.

You're Going to Start Menstruating

Once your breasts start to grow, you'll have your first period about two years after this. This can be a super-scary time, which is why I've dedicated the entire next chapter to it and will aim to answer all the questions you may have. Still, it is a physical thing that will happen to your body.

Feel free to come back to this part of the book at any time, and if something is happening to your body and you don't understand it, take the time to look it up online or ask someone you trust about it. It's not worth getting all worried and stressed out over something very ordinary. Everyone has it, so don't be afraid to ask!

Now, let's get into everything you need to know about the big 'P' word.

Chapter Four: Everything You Need to Know About Periods

Ah, the big 'P' word. You've probably already heard a ton of information about periods. You've heard what they are and what they're not. Apparently, they can feel like nothing, and they can be the biggest, scariest thing in the world. Everybody has their own experiences.

Don't worry, it's scary at first, but once you know what periods are all about, you're going to feel much more confident and much more relaxed with what's going on in your body. This is exactly what this chapter is dedicated too, so if you ever have any questions or you're confused about something, you can always come back to remember again.

So, let's go over the basics.

What is a Period?

A period is the common word used to describe you when your body is going through the menstruation cycle. This is a monthly cycle where blood and the lining of your uterus comes out of your vagina. I know, when I heard this for the first time, I not only thought that was gross, but the work blood made me super worried.

While it's not the most comfortable thing in the world, it doesn't hurt in the way you thought it would. Most people see or hear blood and think, 'oh my god, I'm going to die,' but you won't. It's not a wound, or like you've cut yourself, but more just a trickle of blood that you don't really know about.

Some months, especially as a teenager, you'll come on your period, and you won't even notice until hours later! Before we get into that, let's take a moment to look at the science behind what a period, or the menstruation cycle, really is.

Every month, your body will make eggs that sit in your ovaries. These eggs are used to grow into a baby when you decide to have one later in life. However, if you don't become pregnant, as in you're not having a baby, your body needs to get rid of your eggs, so your body has room to grow new ones.

This process of getting rid of your eggs to make room for new ones to grow is what your period is, and it's why there's tissue (bits of skin) and blood that comes out. This sounds gross, but your entire body is made of blood and tissue, so it's not really any different to your arms or legs!

Every girl has two ovaries, and each one contains an egg. The eggs are so small, and you'll never be able to see them with just your eyes. While your ovary is around the size of an almond nut, it can make between 150,000 and 200,000 eggs per month!

So, every month your body makes eggs, and they sit in your body waiting for a male sperm cell to fertilize it. If it does, you'll become pregnant and will have a baby.

If you don't, your body goes 'okay, there's no baby coming this month, so I don't need these eggs.' The body will then release the lining, which holds the eggs, which will then come out of your vagina. This is all controlled by your hormones, and you won't really feel it at all. However, there are pains that you may feel as your body gets ready to release the eggs.

You may feel bloated, which means you feel like your stomach is really full, like when you need to fart really badly, or you may feel a little pain in your belly, but only on one side. Another sign you may be having your period is called spotting, which is where you'll see a bit of blood in your underwear. This is a great way to tell if you're coming on your period!

Most girls will start their periods around 12-14 years old, and it's really nothing to worry about. It's a completely natural thing to happen, but I understand that it's scary. When I came on my period for the first time, I didn't really know what periods are. Seeing a lot of blood in my underwear was so scary, especially because I was in school and didn't know what to do.

You don't have to go through this yourself, because you're reading this book and you're going to be prepared and will understand all about what periods are and how they work!

How Will I Know When My Period is Coming?

While it happens between the ages of 12 and 14, that's not very helpful when you're trying to stop blood coming out and preparing for the big day. It's also worth saying that while the average age is around 12 to 14, some girls get it at 10. Other girls may get it is as old as 15, both of which are absolutely fine and nothing to worry about.

Some of the best things to look out for include whether you have been wearing a bra for a few years. If you have, then your period is probably on its way. If you have hair under your arms and on your genital areas is another clear sign, and if you have discharge coming out of your vagina.

If you have these things happening to your body, then your period could be coming at any time, so you'll need to make sure you're prepared.

How Can I Be Prepared for My Period?

The most important thing to do is make sure you're carrying out a sanitary towel or tampon around with you wherever you go. Most girls' bathrooms and toilets, especially if you're in school, will have machines that can give you these products. Still, it's always best to carry your own because you don't have to risk making a mess in your pants! You may also want to carry around a pair of underwear in your bag in case it catches you by surprise.

Let's say you're sitting in class, and you feel something happening in your underwear. Your leg may feel a little bit wet, or you may even feel the sensation of thick discharge coming out. When this is happening, you'll want to take your sanitary towel or tampon with you to the bathroom.

Most periods will only last between three to six days per month, but you may feel other symptoms, such as mood swings and tiredness, a few days either side. Don't worry though, while periods will happen every month, they only last until you're between 45 and 55 years old, and then you'll stop having them after you have the menopause, but we won't worry about that too much now as it's a long way off!

How to Use a Sanitary Towel

There are two types of products that can be used to help you get through your period without getting blood everywhere. These are known as sanitary towels and tampons. When you start having periods, I really recommend you use both products in different months and then see which one best suit you.

Some girls find using tampons more comfortable, whereas other girls like using pads (sanitary towels). It's really up to you and what you like to use. It may take a while to get used to using either a pad or a tampon, so it's worth practicing before you have your period, so you know exactly what you're doing when the time goes.

So, how do you use a pad?

Well, most pads will work in the same way. All you do is take a pad out of the packaging and remove the little strips of plastic that cover the pad's sticky parts. Then, all you do is lay the pad out in your underwear and fold the sticky tabs around your underwear, holding the pad in place.

You can then put your underwear back on, and the pad will soak up any blood that comes out of you. You'll want to change your pad at least once a day, maybe a few times a day if you're bleeding a lot. Just check when you go to the bathroom how much you're bleeding, and if you think there's a lot, then just change your pad to a new one.

How to Use a Tampon

Unlike sanitary pads, tampons actually go inside your vagina, which isn't as scary as it sounds. Tampons are made to be super soft and as comfortable as possible. Usually, tampons will come in little plastic or cardboard tubes known as applicators, and it's really up to you which you like best.

Now, there are lots of different tampons brands, so you'll want to follow the instructions included with the box you get. Don't worry, nearly all brands of tampons have made this super easy to read and understand, so just go through the instructions step-by-step, and you'll have it inside you in no time at all.

To give you an idea of what you'll be doing, you push the little applicator inside your vagina in the opening. This is between the urethra, which is where your pee comes out, and your anus, which is where your poop comes out.

Once inside, you pull the applicator out and put it in the bin, and then the tampon, the small cotton bit, will stay inside and will soak up all the blood. You'll also see a bit of white string that comes out of your vagina, and that's just for pulling out the tampon quickly when you're done.

Tampons come in lots of different shapes, sizes, and can soak up blood at different levels. It's all about finding out which ones work best for you, so don't be afraid to give them a go.

Depending on how blood there is, you should change your tampon every four to six hours and replacing it with a new one. One of the biggest fears of using a tampon is getting stuck inside you, which can happen, especially if you're feeling stressed out.

If you ever feel like a tampon is stuck inside you, just relax and wait a few minutes before pulling it out. Make sure you relax because that's probably what's stopping it from coming out!

What Happens If I Don't Have Tampons or Pads?

This happens to every single girl at one point in their lives. It's happened to me loads, and I've heard it happen to many girls, both teenagers, and adult girls. You're going about your day and doing your normal thing, and then suddenly, bam, you feel it. You've come on your period.

You check your bag, and while you thought you had your tampons in there, you don't. So, what do you do?

Well, if you're at home, this shouldn't be a problem because you'll have tampons and pads in the cupboards. If you don't, you'll need to quickly ask mom to go and get you some!

If you're at school, however, that's another matter. It's always good for friends to stick together, so get into a habit of getting your friends to always keep pads and tampons on them. This way, if you or another friend needs one as an emergency, you can always help each other out.

If you're in school or in town, you can go to the toilets, which should have a tampon dispenser you can use. You may also be able to go to the school nurse who should have a supply exactly for this reason, so don't be afraid to ask! If worse comes to worst, or you feel more comfortable doing so, you can always call your mom or dad to come and bring some pads or tampons to you.

Suppose you're in a real emergency, and there's a lot of blood. In that case, you can line your underwear with toilet tissue to help soak up the blood, but this is only going to sort out the problem for a little while, so make sure you get some pads or a tampon as soon as you can!

A lot of girls do tend to get shy or worried about talking to a teacher, friend, or the school nurse about getting a tampon or pad, so if you don't want to say it directly, there are some code phrases you can use.

You may like to say, 'it's that time of the month,' which nearly every adult will then know what you're talking about and will be able to help. You might like to say you need some 'personal things,' and if you're speaking to an adult woman, they're going to know what you mean. As I said before, girls stick together and will help each other in times of need. Puberty and periods are something all women go through, meaning you never have to go through it alone!

Of course, you can stop these emergencies happening in the first place by simply making sure you have spares with you at all times and keep extra spares in your locker or gym bag in case you ever need them!

There's Blood on My Underwear / Trousers/ Pants?!

If your period catches you off guard, you may see that blood has soaked through your underwear and onto your trousers or pants. This does happen from time to time, and if you're at home, it may not be a big deal. Just take off your trousers, put some new ones on, and put the bloody ones in the wash.

If you're at school or in town, this can feel very embarrassing, but it doesn't have to be. If you have a jumper or a jacket, just tie it around your waist until you get home, and there you go, nobody is going to see the blood coming through!

Just make sure as soon as you get home you change your trousers and wash the ones with blood on them. This is important because blood can stain, and you don't want to ruin your clothes. When you start to learn when your period happens every month, then you can be even more prepared and wear dark-colored trousers. Then it doesn't matter if the blood soaks through because nobody is going to see it!

How Do I Track My Periods?

When you want to be as prepared as possible, the most important thing to know is when your period is coming. When you start having your periods, they may seem to go all over the place and arrive at different times, but if you keep an eye on them, they'll start to become more regular over the first few months.

The best thing to do is to write down the date of your period on a piece of paper you can keep somewhere safe, on a calendar, in your diary, or using a period tracking app. Downloading an app on your phone will make it super easy to track the dates of your period, and you'll get little reminders when it's coming, so I really recommend using one if you have a smartphone.

So, let's say you have your first period on the 7Th of August. Write this date down, and then write down the date when you have your next one. It may be on the 9th of September. Do this for a few months, and you should see a common date start appearing. For example, if your date hovered between the 7th and the 9th, you could say your period was starting on the 8th of every month.

When it gets to this time, then you know you need to be extra careful to take tampons or pads with wherever you go, ensuring you're prepared for anything! This may take some getting used to build the habit, but once you've got it, it's a skill you'll keep for life!

Can I Swim on My Period?

This is a great question I'm always asked; can you go swimming when you're on your period? It's a funny image, isn't it? Going into the water and then seeing the blood come out behind you! Okay, it might seem funny or kind of gross, I'll leave that to you to decide, but don't worry, this doesn't have to happen.

If you want to swim while on your period, make sure you're wearing a tampon. If you wear a pad, the pad is just going to fill with water, and it won't work. It has to be a tampon. If you've got a tampon in, you'll all set to go, so go swimming as much as you want!

I Heard Some People Go Crazy on Their Period?

While it can definitely seem and feel like girls go a little crazy during their periods, this is only half true. Due to the load of hormones that will pump throughout your body during this time, you're going to experience mood swings and a different way of thinking. You may feel really angry or really sad, or you may want to cry and spent time by yourself.

If you feel this way and you think there's something wrong with you, don't worry, it's all completely normal, and millions of women feel this way with you every single month. In a following chapter, I'm going to talk about how you can deal with mood swings, not just on your period, but while you're going through puberty in general.

Just know for now that even though you may feel super emotional and intense from time to time, you're allowed to feel like this, but don't believe you're just going crazy; it's just a normal part of growing up. Once your hormones have settled, and puberty is pretty much over, you'll feel much more grounded and at ease with yourself.

How Bad is Period Pain?

There's no doubt that period pain can be some of the worst pain out there, and it will change as you get older. Some girls experience really intense period pains, whereas other girls don't really feel it. You'll probably vary from one to the other as you grow up, so you'll want to make sure you keep an eye on it.

Period pain usually happens right before your period starts, within a week of Day 1, or the first day of your period. You'll normally feel an ache or an uncomfortable pain in your stomach or near your pelvis, and this is normal to have. Pains tend to last around 12 hours but can last several days, both of which are normal.

These pains are actually better known as cramps, or cramping, and is the feeling of your uterus tensing up and releasing as it gets ready for you to have a period. If you feel this pain, then you can do some light stretches or exercise to help get rid of the pain.

You may want to place a hot water bottle over your stomach and stay very still. You just have to find what works for you. Suppose you still feel pain, or the pain is really uncomfortable (more uncomfortable than usual, so see how it feels after several months). In that case, you can take pain relief medication, like Paracetamol or Ibuprofen. Still, it's probably best for your health not to rely on pain killers like this.

Do Periods Ever Stop?

You'll be happy to know that periods don't happen throughout your entire life. There will come a point in your life where you'll reach menopause. This is a word used to describe a point where you can't have babies anymore and therefore won't have periods anymore, but this won't happen until you're around 45 years old or more.

Can I Talk to My Parents About Being on My Period?

Of course, you can! In fact, I highly recommend talking to at least one of your parents as soon as possible about periods and puberty, as long as you can trust them and feel comfortable sharing. If you don't want to share it with them, then you don't have to. All you need to remember is that it's completely your choice.

I would recommend talking to your mom about puberty and periods simply because they have gone through it themselves and will know what it feels like. However, if you want to talk to your dad about it because you feel like you can speak to him easily about it, then go right ahead. It's up to you.

If you have brothers and sisters, you may find they tease you about getting your first period, and that's okay. Just tell them it's a natural part of growing up and that you're going to be an adult very soon!

Chapter Five: Understanding Your Mind During Puberty

We've spoken a lot about how your body will change during your years in puberty, but while there are plenty of obvious signs puberty is happening, there are also some less noticeable changes, such as the ones going on in your mind and brain. There are so many changes that will happen in the way you think, and while this will affect every girl differently, it's good to be aware that the changes are coming.

For starters, you're going to find your likes and dislikes will start to change. You may have really hated a certain type of movie or food before, but you'll try it now and may start to like it. You'll also begin to understand more complex matters, like politics and social structures (like how friend groups work), but this will all come with experience.

The list is actually endless of mind changes that you could go through, but it's common to believe it's going to be a rollercoaster, and it is. There's a reason you'll have heard of so many emotional stories, perhaps from an older friend, relative, or big sister. This is because you're trying to figure out who you are and where your place in the world is.

While it sounds exciting when you put it like this when you're waking up at night and feeling like you want to cry and you don't know why, it can feel very scary, as well as being very lonely. As with everything we've spoken about in this book so far, you don't have to be alone.

Every girl goes through these changes and experiences, so if you can be close with your friends and stick up for each other, you're going to get through it that much easier. However, your friend groups may change a lot as you get older, and that's okay. As your likes and dislikes change, you're going to like and dislike different people and start trying new experiences.

You might go to after-school clubs, or you might go up to a new school and start meeting new and exciting people. This is all very exciting, and you should embrace it with open arms.

Feeling the Pressures of Growing Up

Whether you're starting a new club, moving to a new school, or just trying to figure out who you are, there always seems to be pressure. There's a pressure to make everyone else happy, fit in with your friends, or do well in school. With your body changing and you not really sure with who you are, this can feel like a lot of pressure, and it's probably going to stress you out.

When you add in a lot of strong new emotions that you probably have felt before, then everything is going to seem really crazy and weird. One thing that really worked for me was to start writing a diary or a journal. You might do this already, but I really recommend getting into the habit of journaling every single day, even if you're just writing down some bullet points.

Each day take a moment to write down how you feel. You could write words like 'happy,' 'sad,' 'angry,' or 'in the middle.' Then, try and figure out why you feel the way you do. You might write something like;

Today, I was really sad because mom wouldn't let me go to a friend's house after school. I had done all my homework, and I really wanted to see her new dog, and it made me so mad.

Even writing a small little bit of information like this is a great way to get it out of your mind. This is called venting, and it's a great way to understand how you feel and why you feel the way you do. By writing every day, you'll build up a collection of entries you can look back on at any time.

You can see all the happy and sad times in your life, and if you're feeling really sad, then you can look back and remember all the times you're happy. It's just a really good way of looking after your mental health as you grow up and go through this time of your life.

How to Deal with Mood Swings

Mood swings are super common when you're going through puberty, especially when it comes to being on your period and the weeks leading up to it. It's a weird time. You might wake up in an amazing mood and happier than you've ever been, and then an hour later, you just feel like the worst. This makes you not want to go to school, not want to see anyone, and not want to live your life.

As I said above, one of the best ways to get over these feelings is to keep a diary or journal. Write down your thoughts and feelings, especially when they feel really intense. This way, you can keep track of them and vent them out onto a page.

If a friend or teacher says something and it really annoys you and makes you angry or upset, just write it down in your diary, and you'll feel so much better, only from doing this. You can also make yourself feel better but really looking after yourself. This means eating properly and getting enough exercise, all of which are amazing skills to have and habits that will stay with you throughout your life.

If your mood swings are really bad, and you're finding it incredibly difficult to deal with, you could take a contraception pill or hormone pill. These are pills that you take daily and will stop you from having periods and can also get rid of all your period-related symptoms, like mood swings.

You Can Always Get Support

It doesn't matter what part of puberty you're going through, whether you're dealing with mood swings, suffering form period pains, or just confused about how you feel or what's happening to your body, it's always worth talking to someone about it. You never have to go through it alone.

Talk to someone you can trust, like a parent, teacher, or student nurse, and who will give reliable information. If you don't want to talk to anyone, you can always look for help online on blogs or forums, or find books, like this one! The most important thing to remember is that you're not alone and there is always help out there, no matter what the problem is, as long as you ask for it.

Dealing with Sexual Feelings

As you start getting older and your body starts getting ready through puberty to reproduce, you will begin to experience sexual feelings towards other people. You may feel them towards both boys and girls, or both. This is fine since you're figuring out your own sexuality and where you are in the world.

These sexual feelings are going to bring about physical, emotional, and mental changes that you haven't experienced before, so it's important that you pay attention to them. These feelings are not strange or abnormal, and you'll continue to feel them throughout adult life, especially when you're having sex or making a baby.

However, when you're 9 to 12 years old, you're going to feel these feelings a little bit, and this is what we call 'crushes.' If you've looked at a boy or a girl and felt like you want to be with them, hang out with them all the time, and just want to be close with them, this is what you would call a 'crush.'

You can choose whether you want to keep these feelings private or make them public. No matter what anyone says, it's important that you're making the decision you want to make, so don't be afraid if you need to take some time to think about them. You can always write down your feelings in your diary since this can help you understand them better.

It's worth saying, however, that speaking about your feelings or your crush with a friend or the person you have a crush on may not have the outcome you expect. Your crush might not feel the same way, and that's okay because they're allowed to make their own decisions and feel how they want to feel.

However, suppose the other person does feel the same way. In that case, you could then have a very exciting relationship with that person, so take your time and make the decision you think is best. Remember, you might not have feelings for anyone at all, neither boys nor girls, and that's perfectly normal as well. Just feel how you feel and be aware of what is happening.

If someone approaches you at school or while you're with friends and says they have a crush on you, this can be just as confusing. If you feel the same way, then why not give a relationship or friendship a go and see how you feel. If you don't feel the same way, then it's important to be as kind and as respectful as you can be. Imagine if you had feelings for someone and they didn't feel the same way.

How would you like that person to tell you?

Talking About Masturbation

Masturbation is a natural part of life that you may not think about much now, but the chances are you will as you start to explore your body more. These feelings all come with learning about yourself and understanding what your sexuality is and who you are, which all why puberty is happening in the first place!

Masturbation is where you'll touch yourself on your genital, private areas because it feels good. You may start doing this around 11 or 12 years old and above, and you may enjoy the feelings, or you may feel uncomfortable doing it. Every kid has a different experience and going through puberty and learning about masturbation is all part of going through your puberty journey.

Just to clear a few things up, there is nothing wrong with masturbation, although some religions believe it's not something you should do. Medically and scientifically speaking, there's nothing about masturbation that will harm you in any way. If you want to masturbate or try masturbating, you can, and if you don't want to and it doesn't interest you, then that's fine as well.

If you do want to try it, it's always going to be best if you do it on your own in the privacy of your own house. Take your time and don't rush anything. You may want to talk to your friends about it, which is fine, but remember that this could leave you in a vulnerable position.

Every girl and boy will discover masturbation in their own time, and if it's something other boys and girls don't understand yet, then they may not see it the way you see it. That's okay too, just don't let anybody laugh or bully you over something they don't understand. Learn to understand your sexuality is all about finding out what you want and what you feel comfortable with, not what anybody else says you should feel or think.

Talking About Body Image

As you get older, you're going to start thinking more and more about how your body looks and whether you're happy with what you look like. Perhaps you're already thinking about this, and you feel yourself comparing your body with other girls you know or girls and women you see on the internet.

I know so many young girls about your age who sit and take photos and selfies and use apps to FaceTune themselves and add filters. This is all fine and okay to do, and a natural part of puberty is to look at yourself and compare your body to other girls, but it doesn't come without problems.

The problem is that magazines, television, and the internet are trying to sell you an image of what they think the 'perfect body' looks like. If you look on Instagram or Facebook, and perhaps you even follow some models on there, you see how skinny or curvy they may look, how big their breasts are, or how their faces look.

When you see how many likes and comments their photos get, how much attention they get from girls and boys who think they're really beautiful, it's easy to feel like this is something you want. When you chuck in all the hormones you're feeling from puberty, then these intense feelings get even more intense!

There's only one real way to say this, but there is no perfect body. It just doesn't exist. When you see girls on the TV or on the internet, on Instagram or YouTube, these are not actually what the people look like, but have been edited by people with computers. I know how crazy that sounds, but many people you see on the internet are not even real people, but edited photos of people, just like you edit your pictures with FaceTune or add filters.

The only difference is these photos are edited by professional photo editors who are paid to make the photo look as good as possible! So, if you're scrolling down social media or watching a movie and you think to yourself 'wow, that girl is so beautiful, I want to look like her,' take a moment to remember that this probably isn't what the girl actually looks like, but is an edited version of her.

If you don't believe me, look it up on the internet right now! Take a girl or a woman you follow on social media, perhaps a celebrity, a singer or an actress, and search 'her name without photo editing' and see the images that come up on Google. I'll bet you'll be surprised by how different those women look!

So, when you're looking in the mirror at your changing body, and you feel yourself thinking about how you wish you looked different, like the girls you see on TV or in movies, remember, nobody looks like this. You're trying to look like someone who doesn't exist!

When you're in school or going around your town or city, take a look at everyone who is walking past. You might even be able to see lots of people now out your window. Look at how many different people there are out there. People of all different shapes and sizes and colors and this is beautiful! It's beautiful that everyone gets to look different because we all can be ourselves, rather than all looking like robots and looking the same.

I know this can all sound really confusing, and it may take a couple of years for you to figure this out for yourself but try to take some time to think about what you want to look like. What clothes you want to wear, and whether you want to wear makeup or not. There's really nothing wrong with trying things out and seeing what makes you happy.

The most important thing to remember is to have fun with it. Try lots of different clothes out, not just what your friends are wearing, and see what clothes make you happy. Over time, you'll start to learn what you do and don't like to look like, meaning you can be really happy with what you look like.

We're going through a time in life right now where more girls and women are beginning to accept how we look like as individuals, rather than trying to look like other people, and that's a really positive thing we should all be celebrating!

If you're struggling with your body image, and you're feeling really anxious or depressed with how you look, then don't worry, you're not alone. Thousands, if not millions, of girls go through feeling this way, even when they are adults! The important thing to remember is that you don't need to keep it to yourself if you do feel like this.

You can talk honestly with your parents, friends, teachers, or student nurses, or you may even want to look for advice online that can help you deal with, manage, and understand why you're feeling the way you do.

Just do a little online search for the Kids Advice helpline, or go onto websites like The Butterfly Foundation website, who offer lots of practical body image advice to help you feel better with how you look just being yourself!

A Quick Look into Relationships

We've already spoken a little bit about sexual feelings you may have with yourself or towards other people, and while you may feel a little shy talking about these feelings, having these feelings is a really big part of going through puberty, so it's something we need to talk about!

Sorry if you're reading this book through with your parents!

Many girls and boys will start feeling an attraction towards other boys or girls. This is when you may get sexual feelings towards that other person. You may see them and feel funny and tingly, and you may start thinking about that person all the time.

It's worth saying you may find yourself attracted to boys, other girls, or no one at all, and feeling any of these ways is absolutely fine! Feeling attractions towards someone, or feeling no attractions towards anyone, is healthy and normal. You shouldn't bully or tease anyone else because they feel attracted to different people to who you're attracted to. Everyone can like whoever they want to like.

If you like someone and talk to them about how you feel, you might choose to be in a relationship together, like being girlfriend and boyfriend. This will tend to happen around the age of 12, so for you older kids reading this book, but it's something you'll want to think about.

I could write a whole book on relationships, and how they work and how to make them better, so we'll stick with puberty for this book, but there are some important things to remember.

First, always be open and honest about how you feel. If someone likes you, but you don't like them, you don't have to pretend to like them just so you don't hurt their feelings. Be kind and honest with that other person and let them down gently.

If you like someone and they don't like you in the same way back, that's also okay. Don't take it personally, and just remember that everyone likes different people. You are an amazing, beautiful, and unique girl who can bring so much to the world, so celebrate how unique you are!

There may come a point where you want to be close physically with someone, you're in a relationship with. Remember, laws that state you should only be physically intimate with someone at a certain age, so it's always a good idea to wait until this time. Still, sometimes you may feel like you're ready.

Remember, when it comes to being physical with another person, you need to know that you're comfortable. Make sure you trust the person you're with and that you're comfortable. Don't just be physical with someone else because it will make them happy. Ask yourself if it will make you happy.

If you don't feel comfortable or don't want to do anything, like kissing another person, then remember you don't have to. **You always have a choice.** It's very important to talk with your other person to see how you feel and how they feel. It's important to be open and honest, so you and that other person understand how you feel about each other.

If someone, no matter if they're an adult or another teenager, touches you or kisses you in a way that you don't want them too, you need to make sure you tell them to stop. If they make you feel uncomfortable, pressure you into doing something you don't want to do, or do something to you anyway, you need to talk to someone about it because they are taking away your choice.

It can be scary at first, but it's always important to deal with these situations as soon as possible. Tell a trusted adult if someone has happened to you or look up the websites for information on sexual assault in your local area.

I'll say it one last time to be clear. You always have a choice with what people can and can't do with your body. It is your body. If you want to try something with someone, but then decide you want to stop, you are right to say you don't want to have a choice. Always remember the power you have to do and be who you want to be.

Chapter Six: How to Look After Yourself During Puberty

By now, you should realize that puberty is a very intense and frankly exhausting time to live through. Your body is changing nearly every single day, and your mind is going all over the place. It can be a wonder that we even make it through the other side into adulthood in one piece!

While there's a lot of information in this book to take in, and plenty of experiences you're going to have in the future with it all, it can always be a good idea to look after yourself as best you can.

If you're looking after yourself and making sure you're fit and healthy, you're going to get through puberty in the best possible way, and you're definitely going to be a happier person overall! Throughout this chapter, I'm going to dive into some of the best ways you can look after yourself and how to get through puberty safely in the crazy world we live in.

Eat as Well as You Can

Look, I'm not here to tell you that you can't eat pizza or chocolate. Go ahead and treat yourself to sweets and cake and pasta. You're young and can enjoy yourself! The trick to being healthy and eating well is to not eat these foods all the time. You've probably seen people who are dieting and eating really strict foods on TV or on IG and Facebook and trust me, you don't need to do this.

So many young girls suffer from eating disorders because they see skinny models on the internet who say that this is the right way to be. But when you're naturally, and very healthily, putting on weight because you're going through puberty, you don't need to diet to lose this weight. This is the weight your body needs to have to be healthy!

If you want to be healthy and look after your body, then there are some key points to remember. First, eat a variety of foods. This means not eating lots and lots of sugar, sweets, and chocolate (although a little bit is perfectly fine) and making sure you're eating fruit and vegetables every day.

Also, make sure you're drinking lots of water every single day as well. A really easy way to do this is to get a bottle of water you can take around with you wherever you go. This way, it's really easy to drink more than enough water. You'll notice how much energy doing just this will give you as you'll want to run around more and play as much as you can, rather than feeling tired all the time!

Make Sure You Exercise!

It's getting more and more important for kids like you to exercise to stay fit and healthy. Yeah, I get it. I could easily sit around on my phone or day playing games or browse the internet for hours and hours on my tablet. Still, it's really not healthy to do this, and it always makes me feel real 'blah' when I do.

Instead, put the phone down and get outside! Get some sunlight and run around a bit. A real easy way to do this is to get involved with sports at school or join an after-school club, but I get that not everyone wants to be in the sports team. If sports clubs are not really your thing, then try getting exercise in other areas.

You might even put your headphones in and dance around your bedroom listening to music, and this is exercise! And fun exercise at that! You could go for a walk, maybe even taking your dog for a walk, or just play outside in the garden. The trick is to keep your body moving as much as possible throughout the day.

If you can keep fit and healthy through eating and proper exercise, you'll find you'll be a much happier and calmer person, and facing the difficulties of puberty will be much easier, just because you'll be so much happier as a person!

Keep a Note of Everything

We've spoken a little bit already about the benefits of keeping a diary or journal while you're going through puberty to help you understand yourself and what you're going through a bit better. I'm going to use this space to quickly go into detail of how you can do this properly.

There's no end of benefits that keeping a diary can bring into your life, and it's one of the best ways to be happy with your life. Even adults are finding this out now, so by keeping a diary when you're young, you'll have a skill that can bring you so many positive things in later life!

All you need to do is get yourself a blank notebook and a pen to get started. You could use your computer, the Notes app on your phone, or even a diary app, and if that works for you, then that's great. I personally love using a book and writing by hand because it has a really nice, special feel to it.

When you open your book and go to write, put the date down and write down three things you're grateful for as the first thing you do. This means write down three things that you're really happy with in your life, even if you've had a bad day.

You might be grateful for having your pet, because you love your pet, or might love that you have a certain friend or family. You might really like your teacher, or you're happy that you can see color. There are lots of different things you can be happy about, and no matter how small or big those things are, write them down in your diary.

Once you've done this, start writing about your day. If something happened, write about it. If you've been thinking about something, write it down. If you've been feeling a certain way, are angry about something, or feeling confused, write everything down with as much detail as you can.

Even when you're really happy, try to write down as much information as can you. When you finish this, finish your diary entry by writing down three things you want in life. You might write that you want to be happier, or get good grades, or even just finish your period as early as possible.

No matter what you want in life, write it down. The act of writing everything down in this way every day is a great way to keep your mental wellbeing in check, meaning you'll be happier, less stressed, and less emotional. It's amazing how good just writing things down can make you feel.

However, don't feel like you need to stick with my way of writing things down. If you want to just make bullet points of your day, or only write stuff down that makes your angry, you can do this as well. It's all about finding out what works for you.

Be Prepared

So much of this book has been written in a way to guide you into being prepared. From keeping tampons and pads in your locker and spares in your sports bag to seeing what is coming for you and your sexuality in the future, surviving puberty is about being prepared.

In light of this, make sure you're researching more things you may not understand or want more information on online or reading other books; and there are plenty out there to get started on!

Whether you're buying makeup, shavers, razors, sanitary products, or bras, you can speak to girls and women in your life about their experiences. They can help you with advice on how to choose a bra or where to get certain things.

Some girls will advise you on how to survive relationships with boys, or the best way to ride out period pains. Whatever the advice is, it's always best to listen to other people's experiences and then be prepared to make up your own mind.

I remember my older sister was talking to me about periods, and I was so scared of the pain I thought I was going to feel. After I got my monthly date for when my period was coming, I got prepared with my sister and bought loads of ice cream and chocolate and some Disney DVDs (this was before YouTube and Netflix was a thing).

Then, when my period came, I had everything I needed to curl up on the sofa, eating snacks and watching movies, and it was the best way for me to deal with it. Because I was prepared, going through puberty wasn't a bad thing! It was actually a really enjoyable time.

Can you imagine that?

Chapter Seven: How Puberty Affects Your Skin

I've already spoken a little bit in previous chapters about how going through puberty does a lot for your skin. Not only will you probably, almost certainly, get some acne, but you can also get pimples and spots, and your body is going to be sweating a lot more all over. Unfortunately, all these things are just unavoidable, but it means your skin is going to suffer.

Let me break it down.

Your body is going to be flooded with hormones and chemicals when you start puberty. While this will affect your body in many different ways, one of the main areas it's going to affect is the sebaceous glands. These are the little holes in your skin where your sweat comes out. You can't see these holes because they're so tiny, but they are there. That's why your skin gets wet when you run around and exercise.

On top of letting sweat out of your skin, these glands will produce oils that help keep your skin moisturized and smooth. Try it for yourself. Stroke your arm now and feel how soft it is, and then stroke your parent's arm. Can you tell the difference in how smooth your skin is compared to theirs? This is all thanks to these little glands!

However, when you start going through puberty, these little glands go into overdrive mode and make lots and lots of oil at the same time. This oil is called 'sebum,' just in case you were wondering. This sebum you produce when you're in puberty is much thicker than normal sebum from when you're a small kid, which means it can block up the holes in your skin.

This is how pimples and spots are made!

If there are lots and lots of sebum (skin oil), and the pimple becomes inflamed, this is when you'll get lots of pimples, and this is called acne. You'll mostly get acne when you become a teenager, so when you're about 13 years old and above, and acne can come and go for several years.

Don't worry, when you get spots and pimples, it can really feel like the end of the world. Trust me, I've been there. I had so many spots and pimples on my face when I was a teenager, and I thought I was really ugly. I know what you're thinking, Eww, that's gross to have so many spots and stuff, but that's just how it is.

When I was 17, my spots cleared up, and I had really good skin until now, which makes me feel really comfortable and happy in my body now! What I didn't realize is that I could have clean, spot-free skin when I was going through puberty. All you need to do is follow the advice in the next section!

Bonus: Skin Care Tips You Need to Know

Looking after your skin, so you don't have as many spots and pimples, is so easy, and all it takes is just being a little be aware of how you're living your life. You may think 'hey, I don't have spots and pimples, so I don't need to read this section,' but I bet you're going to get some at some point, especially over the next few years, so it's always a good idea to know how to get rid of them!

Let's not waste any more time and get straight into it!

Why is Looking After Your Skin Important?

If you're wondering why we're even bothering to look after our skin, let me tell you there are lots of reasons! Yes, going through puberty means you're going to get pimples and spots of some kind, but if you can look after your skin, then you're going to get fewer spots and fewer chances of getting acne.

There's nothing wrong with having acne, but it can be a bit of a blow to your confidence and can leave you feeling kind of bad about yourself when you look in the mirror and then have to go to school. If you look after your skin, you're going to feel better and more confident in yourself, which means you'll be happier and more loving towards the world.

This is especially important while going through puberty because your hormones can make you feel so emotional. Any bad feelings you have about yourself can feel ten times bigger than they are!

So, by looking after your skin, you're doing two things. One, you're helping your skin look clean and fresh and stay healthy, which is going to make you feel really good about yourself. You'll see your friends and go to school, and you'll feel happy to be there, rather than sad that you're trying to hide your spots all the time.

Secondly, you're going to give yourself healthy skin. The world is full of bad chemicals in the air, which is really unhealthy for your skin. Getting yourself a proper skincare routine now means you're going to have a proper skincare routine for the rest of your life. It's a skill you'll keep with you as an adult for many years to come!

The Basics of Looking After Your Skin

As a general rule, you should be cleaning up and looking after your skin every single day. You can do this once in the morning once you wake up, and once at night before you go to bed, just by washing your face with warm water and a bit of soap. Try to not use any super-strong soap as this can actually damage your skin!

Remember the glands and oils we were talking about in the last chapter? Well, while pimples and spots are caused by lots of oil, your skin still needs some oil to be healthy, so you don't want to wash it all away. We're just washing away the amount of oil that your skin doesn't need.

The really easy way to do this is to fill up the sink in your bathroom with warm water, making sure it's not too hot that you're going to burn your skin! Using a flannel or washcloth, make the cloth really wet, ring out the excess water, and then wash your face with it, making sure you go across your forehead and all around the sides by your cheeks. Your parents can help you do this properly, making sure you don't miss anywhere!

Then, once you've washed your face correctly, dry all the water off with a clean towel. While dirt doesn't actually make pimples, it's only the sebum gland oil that does, it's always better to have a clean face.

Try to get into the routine of washing your face as the first thing you do when you wake up in the morning. This is because all the oil and sweat from hours of sleeping have built up overnight and have collected on your skin. You want to get rid of this stuff as soon as possible!

Avoid using soap in the mornings, but instead use a cleansing product. Remember not to rub your skin too hard since this can cause your skin to become red and irritated and increase the oils in your skin, leading to more spots and acne, so be gentle with yourself!

Finding Your 'Skin Type'

Every girl and boy has a different skin type. I know, this sounds like it's going to make everything super confusing but bear with me. While everybody produces sebum, we all produce it in different amounts naturally, which means some girls have oily skin, and other girls have dry skin. Other girls will sit somewhere in the middle.

You can't look after your skin properly if you don't know your skin type, so let's figure it out.

If you have Normal Skin, this means your skin is fairly soft and very smooth. The oils and water your skin produces and lets out are pretty balanced, and you don't really have any patches of dry skin.

If this is your skin type, make sure you keep up with the basic skincare we spoke about above and use a moisturizer to make sure your skin doesn't dry out and crack, which isn't as bad as it sounds. It just means you'll get little lines on your face.

If you have oily skin, your skin may look shinier than other people's skin, and you probably have more blackheads, pimples, acne, and whiteheads than some other people. Don't worry, most kids and teenagers going through puberty will have skin like this at some point because of hormones, but you may have naturally oily skin, which makes these spots worse than normal.

If you have oily skin, make sure you're using soap and water to thoroughly clean and wash your face at least two times a day (once in the morning and once at night), and maybe even three times if you find your skin is really oily. You may also want to use cleansing pads to help clear out your extra sebum pores that are collecting there.

If you have dry skin, you'll find your skin is a little bit flakier than most people's skin, and it feels dry when you touch it. You may also find your skin is itchy and dull and make peel in places.

If you have dry skin, make sure you don't wash your face and skin with soap, but instead use water and a mild strength cleansing product. Don't wash or scrub your face too much as this will get rid of the natural oils your face needs! You may even just want to wash your face once a day before bed and use a moisturizer to stop your skin from drying out throughout the day.

Avoid Makeup Powders

If you have particularly oily skin, you may want to get rid of the shine using a makeup powder, but this can be a bad idea. While powder can make your skin shine a little less intense, the powder can get into your pores and block them up. As you know, when the pores get blocked full of oil, this is where spots and acne is going to turn up!

Instead, the best way to reduce the shine of your skin is to dab your face with a tissue or a cleansing pad. Just dab your skin gently in patches, holding the pad to your face for a few seconds and then moving it around your face. This will pick up the oil without spreading it around your face and won't block your pores!

Be Careful with Your Makeup

While we're on the subject of makeup, don't worry, I'm not about to preach that you shouldn't wear any makeup and it's bad for your skin. You're a kid, and you're going to want to try makeup at some point and see what you like and don't like, and that's fine. What you do need to do, however, is make sure you're keeping your face clean and healthy!

If you're wearing makeup in the day, make sure you're washing it off at night and then cleansing your face using your everyday skincare routine. If you use makeup brushes, make sure you're cleaning the brushes regularly, perhaps once a week, depending on how often you're using them.

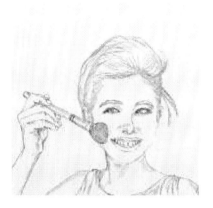

The only makeup I would avoid using when you're younger is foundation because this can be very heavy on the skin and can block pores, which leads to acne. However, you can instead use a skin-tinted moisturizer that works in the same way as a foundation, but it's much better for your skin.

Just make sure you're choosing the right shade of moisturizer to match your skin color!

Think About Your Diet

We spoke about this a little bit in the last chapter, but the foods you're eating play a huge part in whether you get lots of acne and spots or not. The worst foods are sugary foods, like sweets, cake, and chocolate, and certain kinds of fatty foods, like pizzas and takeaways.

I'll repeat this just we're clear but eating some chocolate or having a pizza with your friends will not make you break out with a lot of acne and spots but eating these kinds of foods all the time will. Dairy products are also known to be very common causes of acne, so try to avoid drinking a ton of milk and eating a lot of cheese.

If you're trying to manage your diet and you keep getting spots and acne, it may be a good idea to keep a food diary. You can then see what foods you're eating and when you're getting spots come up, therefore allowing you to see which foods are causing you to get spots. If you're still struggling to figure it out, you may want to take an allergy test!

Try to stick with eating lots of healthy foods, like fruits and vegetables, and drinking lots of water throughout the day, as this is easily the best way to look after your skin and to make sure it's as clean and clear from spots and pimples as possible.

Don't Touch Your Spots!

I know, I get it. Not touching or squeezing your spots is really difficult, and there's nothing more satisfying, or grosser, than squeezing a spot and seeing all that yucky stuff come out. Some girls love squeezing them, and some girls hate it. Either way, it's always best to leave your spots alone and let them heal on their own.

I know this can be so difficult. When you look in the mirror and see a spot, there's nothing else you want to do that squeeze it and pop it and hope it goes away but squeezing your pimples like this don't actually help. It actually makes the spot worse!

When you squeeze spots and pimples, you're causing all that excess oil (sebum) to come out and spread onto other parts of your face. If you have excess sebum on your hands and fingers when you're squeezing the spots, then you're just putting more oil back into your face, which will give you even more pimples!

As well as making your spots worse, if you squeeze them too many times or squeeze the spots too hard, then you can even create scars on your face. These will only be small scars (about the size of the spot), but these scars won't go away easier, and you may even have them for the rest of your life!

So, with all this information, it's easy to see that when you get spots and pimples, it's always best just to leave them alone and try to ignore them as much as possible. I know this can be hard, and you just want to get rid of them as quickly as possible, but the best way to do this is to leave them alone and let them heal on their own, no matter how hard that might be.

In general, it's important to just not touch your face as much as you can. Your hands touch all kinds of things throughout the day and collect all sorts of bacteria and germs. Think about how many people in your school touch your textbooks and tables, and where their hands may have been! Now think about all those germs that have then gone onto your hand, and then go onto your face.

Yuck!

Try, as much as you can, to not touch your face, or at least always wash your hands before touching your face. You'll also want to avoid sharing makeup products with your friends, because you're just passing the germs and bacteria around!

Exfoliate Your Skin!

A personal favorite of mine.

Exfoliating your skin means to clear your skin of dead skin cells that may have built up and help keep your skin smooth and soft. If you can look after your skin in this way now, then you're going to have lots of soft and smooth skin when you're an adult, which is what so many adults wish they had!

Try to avoid using exfoliation products from a store because these will be so strong on your delicate skin. Instead, you can make your own, and this is much more fun! Just mix sugar and honey together into a bowl and apply it to your face. It may feel a bit weird at first, but this is all you need to do.

If you have sensitive, soft skin, if you can instead use milk and honey mixed with oatmeal. This is a lot of fun to do with friends; just make sure you wash it all off thoroughly afterward!

Use Sunscreen

The sun can so quickly burn your skin, and the harmful UV rays can do so much damage. It may not seem like it at the time, but when you're in the sun for many years as a teenager, you'll start to see the effects in later life, so don't risk it!

You're basically never too young to wear sunscreen, which is why your parents should have made you wear it when you were little! Now you're a bit older, it's time to start looking after your own skin, so put some sunscreen on before you go out in hot, sunny weather.

Keep some with you while you're at school, maybe in your school bag or locker, so it's easily available whenever you need some!

Get Professional Help

If your spots and acne are getting worse and worse, and it's really making you feel sad about yourself, you can get medical help from a doctor who can put you on a treatment plan. These plans can vary a lot and may involve using some sort of cream every day to help treat your spots, or you may have an operation.

The operation isn't a scary one and is only really used if you have really bad acne, or it's making you feel really bad about yourself, so the chances are you're not going to need it but know that it does exist.

If you feel really bad about your acne, are getting bullied for it, or it's making you feel really sad, then speak to an adult you can trust. This could be your parent, your teacher, or your school nurse. They will help you figure out ways of dealing with how you're feeling, and if you're still not feeling better, then helping you to see a doctor who will be able to talk about your options.

However, most teenagers won't need to go this far, but remember it's available if you really, really need it.

Final Thoughts

And there we go! That about wraps up this book on what to expect when you're heading into puberty. I know this is all a lot of information to take in, and there's so much complicated stuff to think about; it may all seem a little overwhelming, but don't worry, you'll get it.

I'm hoping that the words in this book have made you feel a lot more confident in yourself and your body, and that you're prepared for anything that may come your way! Puberty doesn't have to be a big, scary time of your life. It can be fun and exciting, as long as you know what's heading your way and how to be prepared for it all!

If you ever find yourself with any questions, or you're not sure about something, feel free to come back to this book at any time and look up the answer online or in other books, or talk to someone you can trust. It's so important to remember that you're never alone going through puberty, and it's something every girl and boy goes through at some point in their lives.

Talk about things that concern you with your friends and other girls in your school. Some girls may not have read this book and may be really scared about what they're going through, and you may be able to help them feel better about what's going on.

It's really important to remember that every girl is going through their own experience of puberty, and it's really not nice to laugh or pick on other girls who may be putting on more weight, have bigger breasts, or may have lots of acne, for example. Nobody wants to be bullied by other people, let alone other girls. Try to be as kind and as helpful as possible, because if puberty gives you lots of acne or weight, you wouldn't want other girls to bully you.

Finally, if you enjoyed reading this book and found it really helpful, don't forget to leave a positive review online. This really helps me out because I get to see how helpful you found it, and it keeps me inspired to write more!

Good luck young woman of the world, with everything you go through in life, and good luck with puberty! The fact you've picked up and read this book tells me you're serious about learning about how your body works and how to deal with everything that's going to happen in the future, so you've already taken a big step; a step that many girls will never even think about doing, so you should feel strong and proud of yourself for doing just that!

Being responsible for your mind and body, like you have been by reading this book, is what will make you into a responsible, kind, and educated adult, no matter what you end up doing with your life. Be excited. Be happy. Be confident in yourself and believe anything is possible!

You deserve the best!

Disclaimer

This book contains opinions and ideas of the author and is meant to teach the reader informative and helpful knowledge while due care should be taken by the user in the application of the information provided. The instructions and strategies are possibly not right for every reader and there is no guarantee that they work for everyone. Using this book and implementing the information/recipes therein contained is explicitly your own responsibility and risk. This work with all its contents, does not guarantee correctness, completion, quality or correctness of the provided information. Misinformation or misprints cannot be completely eliminated.

Printed in Great Britain
by Amazon